CELEBRATING THE NAME MARY

Celebrating the Name Mary

Walter the Educator

Silent King Books a WhichHead Imprint

Copyright © 2024 by Walter the Educator

All rights reserved. No part of this book may be reproduced in any manner whatsoever without written permission except in the case of brief quotations embodied in critical articles and reviews.

First Printing, 2024

Disclaimer
This book is a literary work; poems are not about specific persons, locations, situations, and/or circumstances unless mentioned in a historical context. This book is for entertainment and informational purposes only. The author and publisher offer this information without warranties expressed or implied. No matter the grounds, neither the author nor the publisher will be accountable for any losses, injuries, or other damages caused by the reader's use of this book. The use of this book acknowledges an understanding and acceptance of this disclaimer.

dedicated to everyone with the first name of Mary

"Earning a degree in chemistry changed my life and gave me a respect for the discipline of poetry!" - Walter the Educator

Chemistry and poetry may seem disparate, yet a nuanced exploration reveals an intriguing interplay between the empirical realm of molecules and the ethereal domain of verses. At first glance, chemistry delves into the molecular tapestry of existence, unraveling the secrets of elements and compounds. Conversely, poetry ventures into the boundless realms of emotions and imagination, weaving linguistic tapestries that transcend the physical confines.

Upon closer inspection, parallels emerge. Both disciplines involve a meticulous dance of elements—whether in the periodic table or the rhythmic patterns of language. The periodicity of elements resonates with the cadence of poetic meter, each element possessing a unique identity akin to the distinct essence of words. Chemical reactions, akin to the fusion of words in verses, engender transformative experiences.

Metaphors and similes, intrinsic to poetic expression, find an unexpected ally in chemistry's ability to draw parallels between disparate phenomena. The alchemy of language mirrors the transformative processes witnessed in chemical reactions, where the mundane metamorphoses into the extraordinary.

In essence, chemistry and poetry converge at the crossroads of creativity, where one seeks the essence of matter, and the other, the essence of expression. The alchemical union of these seemingly divergent realms births a synthesis of understanding, inviting us to perceive the world through the kaleidoscopic lens of both science and art.

CONTENTS

Dedication v

One - Mary, A Name 1

Two - Legacy Of Love 3

Three - Symphony Of Grace 5

Four - Harmony Of Hope 7

Five - Whispered Prayer 9

Six - Makes Us Whole 11

Seven - Sublime 13

Eight - Cosmic Hands 15

Nine - Tranquil And Still 17

Ten - Embracing All 19

Eleven - Forever Endear 21

Twelve - Reverie Of Letters 23

Thirteen - Timeless Sonnet 25

Fourteen - Gentle And Bright 27

Fifteen - Poetic Dream 29

Sixteen - Mary, The Opus 31

Seventeen - Garden Of Thought 33

Eighteen - Eternally Blessed 35

Nineteen - You Stand 37

Twenty - Mary's Light 39

Twenty-One - Mary's Melody Rings 41

Twenty-Two - Soaring High 43

Twenty-Three - Sing Of Mary 45

Twenty-Four - Ageless Youth 47

Twenty-Five - Celebrated Adored And Adored 49

Twenty-Six - Magnificent And Majestic . . . 51

Twenty-Seven - Precious Pearl 53

Twenty-Eight - Pure And Rare 55

Twenty-Nine - Hail To Thee 57

Thirty - Million Stars 59

Thirty-One - Regal Beauty 61

Thirty-Two - Love And Peace 63

Thirty-Three - Boundaries Of Time 65

Thirty-Four - Day And Night 67

Thirty-Five - Haven Of Hope 69

About The Author 71

ONE

MARY, A NAME

In the hush of twilight's gentle glow,
Resides a name that all should know,
Mary, a name of timeless grace,
In every heart, a sacred place.

Like whispers of a tranquil stream,
Her name evokes a peaceful dream,
A melody that softly sings,
Of love that spreads on angel wings.

In tales of old and legends spun,
Mary's name, a chosen one,
A symbol of hope and faith so true,
Guiding hearts to skies of azure blue.

In gardens where the lilies grow,
Her name dances with a radiant glow,
A beacon of light in darkest night,
A compass true, a steadfast might.

So let us raise our voices high,
And praise the name that paints the sky,
Mary, a name that stands apart,
Engraved forever in every heart.

For in this world of joy and woes,
Her name brings solace, love, and rose,
Mary, a name of timeless grace,
In every soul, a sacred place.

TWO

LEGACY OF LOVE

Amidst the stars and boundless sky,
There dwells a name that's lifted high,
Mary, a name that echoes through time,
A symphony of grace, pure and prime.

In fields of gold and meadows green,
Her name blooms bright, a wondrous scene,
A tapestry of dreams untold,
In every whisper, a story unfolds.

From ancient halls to modern streets,
Mary's name, a melody that beats,
A rhythm of strength and gentle might,
A beacon of hope in the darkest night.

In every smile and tender gaze,
Her name ignites a warming blaze,
A legacy of love and endless care,
In every heart, a treasure rare.

So let us honor with every breath,
The name of Mary, conquering death,
For in her name, we find our way,
Through stormy seas and sunlit day.
    Mary, a name that forever rings,
In every soul, her spirit sings,
Majestic Mary, a name of power and grace,
In every life, a sacred place.

THREE

SYMPHONY OF GRACE

Mary, oh maiden of the morning dew,
Thy name doth sing a melody so true,
A symphony of grace, a dance of light,
In every syllable, a star so bright.
  Majestic Mary, mistress of the meadows,
In thy name, a garden of lilies and shadows,
A tapestry of dreams, a river's gentle flow,
Each letter a blossom, each sound a soft echo.
  Marvelous Mary, muse of the moonlit night,
In thy name, a sonnet of love takes flight,
A whisper in the wind, a secret in the sea,
Each verse a treasure, each note a melody.
  Mystical Mary, mirror of the mountain's might,
In thy name, a painting of colors so bright,
A rainbow in the rain, a flame in the sky,
Each stroke a story, each hue a lullaby.

Oh, Mary, maiden of the timeless tale,
In thy name, a legend that will never pale,
A legacy of love, a legacy of light,
In every heartbeat, thy name shines so bright.
　Mary, oh maiden of the morning dew,
Thy name doth sing a melody so true,
A symphony of grace, a dance of light,
In every syllable, a star so bright.

FOUR

HARMONY OF HOPE

Majestic Mary, maiden of the misty moors,
In your name, a symphony of secrets soars,
A tapestry of time, a whisper in the wind,
Each syllable a serenade, a story to rescind.
Marvelous Mary, mistress of the midnight sky,
In your name, a dance of dreams takes flight on high,
A constellation of hope, a comet's fiery trail,
Each letter a lighthouse, each sound a sacred sail.
Mystical Mary, muse of the mountain's might,
In your name, a melody of magic takes flight,
A reverie in the rain, a riddle in the stars,
Each verse a voyage, each note a nebula afar.
Oh, Mary, maiden of the moonlit reverie,
In your name, a waltz of wonder waltzes free,
A legacy of light, a legacy of love,
In every heartbeat, your name ascends above.

Mary, oh maiden of the meadow's gentle hue,
In your name, a sonnet of serenity rings true,
A harmony of hope, a haven for the heart,
In every whispered word, your name becomes an art.

FIVE

WHISPERED PRAYER

Majestic Mary, a melody of morning mist,
In your name, a tapestry of tranquility exists,
A symphony of serenity, a sanctuary of soul,
Each syllable a serendipity, a sacred scroll.

Marvelous Mary, mistress of the midnight moon,
In your name, a reverie of radiance is in bloom,
A constellation of courage, a cascade of grace,
Each letter a lighthouse, each sound a solace in space.

Mystical Mary, muse of the mountain's majesty,
In your name, a mural of mystery, a masterpiece, a symphony,
A reverie in the rain, a rhapsody in the wind,
Each verse a voyage, each note a nebula within.

Oh, Mary, maiden of the moonlit melody,
In your name, a legacy of love and liberty,

A melody of hope, a haven for the heart,
In every whispered word, your name becomes an art.
    Mary, oh maiden of the meadow's gentle glow,
In your name, a sonnet of solace begins to flow,
A harmony of healing, a hymn of hope and grace,
In every whispered prayer, your name becomes a sacred space.

SIX

MAKES US WHOLE

Majestic Mary, mistress of the morning mist,
In your name, a symphony of serenity persists,
A melody of moonbeams, a tapestry of time,
Each syllable a sanctuary, each sound a sacred chime.

Marvelous Mary, muse of the midnight sky,
In your name, a rhapsody of radiance flies high,
A constellation of courage, a cascade of dreams,
Each letter a lantern, each note a nimbus that gleams.

Mystical Mary, maiden of the mountain's might,
In your name, a mosaic of magic takes flight,
A reverie in the rain, a rhythm in the wind,
Each verse a voyage, each whisper a waltz that's twinned.

Oh, Mary, maiden of the moonlit reverie,
In your name, a legacy of love sets hearts free,
A melody of hope, a harbor for the heart,

In every whispered word, your name becomes a work of art.

    Mary, oh maiden of the meadow's gentle grace,
In your name, a sonnet of solace finds its place,
A harmony of healing, a haven for the soul,
In every whispered prayer, your name makes us whole.

SEVEN

SUBLIME

In the realm of names, Mary reigns supreme,
A melody of letters, a poetic dream.
Her syllables dance in a celestial ballet,
Echoing through time, an eternal display.
    Majestic Mary, a symphony of grace,
In every letter, a delicate embrace.
Mirthful in M, a beginning so bright,
A radiant dawn, a sunlit flight.
    A in her name, an arc of allure,
A gentle whisper, a love pure.
R unfolds like petals in bloom,
A fragrant garden, dispelling gloom.
    Y, the finale, a crescendo of sound,
In Mary's essence, beauty profound.

A serenade of letters, harmonious and sweet,
A poetic ode, her name a heartbeat.
    Celestial Mary, celestial light,
In galaxies of letters, shining bright.
A cosmic dance, a celestial rhyme,
In the vast cosmos, Mary, sublime.

EIGHT

COSMIC HANDS

In the tapestry of names, Mary weaves,
A symphony of letters, a spell that conceives.
Majestic Mary, a regal refrain,
Her name, a cascade of gentle rain.

M, the monarch of her title,
A crown of grace, a regal recital.
A in her name, an anthem of art,
A canvas of dreams, a masterpiece's start.

R unfolds like petals in the dawn,
A blossom of strength, a spirit reborn.
Y, the echo of a distant melody,
A lullaby whispered by destiny.

In Mary's realm, the moonlight weaves,
A nocturnal sonnet, as the night conceives.
Her name, a constellation in the cosmic sea,
A celestial ballet, an eternal decree.

Marvelous Mary, in syllables spun,
A sonnet unsung, yet never undone.
In the lexicon of elegance, her name stands,
A poetic tapestry woven by cosmic hands.

NINE

TRANQUIL AND STILL

Mary, a sonnet stitched in time's embrace,
Her name, a prism, casting hues of grace.
In the garden of letters, she blooms,
A melody of petals, where poetry looms.

M, the maestro, a conductor's wand,
Guiding verses in an enchanting bond.
A in her name, an aurora's glow,
A whispered promise, a river's flow.

R, a phoenix rising from the ink,
Feathers of resilience, in verses link.
Y, the twilight, a soft adieu,
A cosmic lullaby, woven through.

Her name, a voyage in celestial seas,
Navigating verses with gentle ease.
In the tapestry of language, she's spun,
A lyric unsung, yet never undone.

Mary, a serenade in moonlit nights,
A constellation of poetic delights.
Her name, an echo in the poet's quill,
A timeless sonnet, tranquil and still.

TEN

EMBRACING ALL

Mary, a melody in the symphony of existence,
A lyrical dance, a poetic insistence.
In the lexicon of grace, her name prevails,
A tapestry woven with celestial tales.

M, a mountain standing tall,
A beacon of strength, a celestial hall.
A in her name, an aurora's glow,
A sunrise whispering tales of long ago.

R, a river meandering through time,
A journey of resilience, a rhythm sublime.
Y, the yearning of a distant song,
A melody in the cosmic throng.

In Mary's name, constellations align,
A celestial sonnet, where stars entwine.
Her name, an anthem in nature's hymn,
A verse unfolding, serene and prim.

    Majestic Mary, in syllables spun,
A poem unsung, yet never undone.
In the cosmic library, her name inscribed,
A celestial parchment, forever described.
    A dance of letters, a ballet in rhyme,
Mary, the muse in the poet's clime.
Her name, a lyric in time's grand ball,
A poetic sonnet, embracing all.

ELEVEN

FOREVER ENDEAR

Mary, a melody etched on the parchment of the soul,
A sonnet unfolding, a tapestry unroll.
In the gallery of names, she's a masterpiece,
A poetic ballet, where elegance will never cease.
M, a moonrise in the twilight sky,
A luminous beacon, catching every eye.
A in her name, an aurora's glow,
A symphony of colors in a rhythmic flow.
R, a river winding through the poetic land,
A serenade of verses, crafted by skilled hands.
Y, the yonder where dreams take flight,
A constellation of wishes, sparkling in the night.
In the ballad of Mary, each letter hums,
A lyrical journey where the spirit drums.

Her name, a garden where metaphors bloom,
A poetic sanctuary, dispelling all gloom.
   Majestic Mary, in the lexicon of grace,
A celestial dance, a timeless embrace.
Her name, a voyage on the cosmic sea,
A harmonious melody, wild and free.
   In the sonnet of existence, Mary's a refrain,
A verse unspoken, yet not in vain.
Her name, a whisper in the poet's ear,
A symphony of words that forever endear.

TWELVE

REVERIE OF LETTERS

    Mary, a sylvan sonnet in nature's embrace,
Her name, a cascade of leaves in a tranquil race.
In the arboreal alphabet, she stands tall,
A whispering willow, a serenade in the fall.
    M, the moonlight weaving her name,
A nocturnal dance, a celestial flame.
A in her name, an aurora's birth,
A kaleidoscope of dreams, a canvas of worth.
    R unfolds like petals in morning's glow,
A floral tapestry, a sunrise tableau.
Y, the yearning of a nightingale's song,
A melody in the breeze, where dreams belong.
    In Mary's name, a symphony takes flight,
Notes pirouetting in the moonlit night.
Her name, an echo in the forest's refrain,
A woodland sonnet, untouched by disdain.

Majestic Mary, in the heart's serenade,
A cascade of verses, a poetic cascade.
Her name, a river winding through the soul,
A rhythmic poem where emotions stroll.
　　In the poetry of existence, Mary's a theme,
A reverie of letters, a tranquil stream.
Her name, a lullaby in the poet's quill,
A tranquil verse that time can't distill.

THIRTEEN

TIMELESS SONNET

Mary, a celestial sonnet on life's grand stage,
A lyrical whisper, an eternal page.
In the cosmic ballroom, she waltzes with grace,
A poetic ballet, a timeless embrace.

M, a moonbeam in the velvet night,
A luminescent journey, gentle and bright.
A in her name, an aurora's glow,
A tapestry of colors in a rhythmic flow.

R, a river weaving through the heart's expanse,
A serenade of echoes, a poetic dance.
Y, the yearning of a distant refrain,
A symphony of dreams in the cosmic terrain.

In Mary's name, constellations align,
A celestial dance, where stars entwine.
Her name, an anthem in the universe's hymn,
A verse unfolding, serene and prim.

Majestic Mary, in the lexicon of dreams,
A tapestry woven with celestial beams.
Her name, a melody in time's grand ball,
A poetic sonnet, embracing all.

In the mosaic of letters, she finds her place,
A poetic serenity, a name to embrace.
Mary, the muse in the poet's quill,
A timeless sonnet, echoing still.

FOURTEEN

GENTLE AND BRIGHT

Mary, a luminescent echo in the tapestry of time,
Her name, a poetic paradigm, a celestial chime.
In the lexicon of elegance, she reigns,
A symphony of syllables, where serenity remains.
    M, a moonlit voyage in the midnight sea,
A celestial dance, a nocturnal decree.
A in her name, an aurora's gentle hue,
A canvas of dreams, where fantasies accrue.
    R unfolds like petals in the dawn's embrace,
A floral sonnet, a sunrise grace.
Y, the yearning of a nightingale's song,
A melody in the zephyr, where dreams belong.
    In Mary's realm, constellations converse,
A cosmic ballad, where verses immerse.

Her name, an anthem in the celestial choir,
A lyrical resonance that will never tire.
    Majestic Mary, in the poet's quill,
A sonnet untold, a verse to distill.
Her name, a melody woven in cosmic art,
A symphony that echoes from the heart.
    In the poetry of existence, Mary's the theme,
A luminous sonnet, a moonlit dream.
Her name, a serenade in the starlit night,
A celestial whisper, gentle and bright.

FIFTEEN

POETIC DREAM

Mary, a serendipitous sonnet in life's ballet,
Her name, a melody, a sunlit array.
In the lexicon of grace, she's a gentle breeze,
A poetic journey through enchanted trees.

M, a mosaic of moonbeams in the night,
A luminary dance, a celestial light.
A in her name, an aurora's tender glow,
A canvas of dreams where fantasies flow.

R unfolds like petals in dawn's embrace,
A floral tapestry, a sunrise grace.
Y, the yearning of a nightingale's song,
A melody in the breeze, where dreams belong.

In Mary's name, constellations conspire,
A cosmic ballad, where stars acquire.
Her name, an anthem in the universe's choir,
A poetic resonance, a celestial fire.

Majestic Mary, in the poet's quill,
A verse untold, a tranquil thrill.
Her name, a river flowing through the soul,
A lyrical sonnet where emotions stroll.

In the grand symphony of existence, Mary's a note,
A harmonic resonance, gently afloat.
Her name, a serenade in the twilight's gleam,
A celestial whisper, a poetic dream.

SIXTEEN

MARY, THE OPUS

In realms of reverie, where whispers weave,
A name adorned with grace, oh, Mary, believe!
Her moniker, a melody in life's grand score,
A symphony of elegance, forevermore.
    In twilight's tender hues, she blossoms bright,
A celestial ballet, pure celestial light.
Mary, the muse, in gardens of words,
Where petals of prose, in harmony, gird.
    Amidst the cosmic tapestry, she twirls,
A dance of constellations, as stardust swirls.
Her name, an aurora in the poetic night,
Painting verses with celestial delight.
    Oh, Mary, the oracle of tales untold,
In the parchment of destiny, your name's enrolled.

A sonnet in the zephyr, a lyrical cascade,
In the lexicon of dreams, your essence laid.
    Through epochs and echoes, your name resounds,
In the emerald meadows and enchanted mounds.
Mary, the echo in eternity's ear,
A serenade of syllables, forever near.
    In the kaleidoscope of linguistic art,
Mary, the opus, a masterpiece to impart.
Her name, a quill in the poet's hand,
In the anthology of existence, forever to stand.

SEVENTEEN

GARDEN OF THOUGHT

In the tapestry of time, a name blooms divine,
Mary, a sonnet sung by the cosmic design.
Her syllables pirouette in the starry ballet,
A celestial ballad, where dreams find their way.

In the garden of verses, Mary takes flight,
A phoenix of prose, igniting the night.
Her name, a lullaby in the moon's tender embrace,
Whispered by zephyrs, adorned with grace.

Majestic Mary, in the lexicon's embrace,
A mosaic of meanings, a linguistic trace.
Each letter, a brushstroke in the canvas of sound,
A symphony of echoes, forever unbound.

Her essence, a chiaroscuro of hues,
Painting the horizon with poetic clues.
In the alchemy of words, a mystical potion,
Mary, the enchantress, stirs the ocean.

A sonnet unfurls in the garden of thought,
Where Mary's name, a tapestry sought.
Harmonizing with echoes in the poet's plea,
A perennial anthem, ever free.

Oh, Mary, in the cathedral of language, you stand,
A cornerstone of verses, meticulously planned.
A celestial dance of letters in the poet's domain,
Mary, the muse, an eternal refrain.

EIGHTEEN

ETERNALLY BLESSED

    In the lexicon's ballroom, Mary takes the lead,
A waltz of syllables, a linguistic deed.
Her name, a serenade whispered by the breeze,
Echoes of elegance through the enchanted trees.
    Majestic Mary, in the script of fate,
A lyric woven in threads ornate.
Each consonant, a dancer in the cosmic ballet,
A poetic rhapsody that never fades away.
    In the tapestry of dreams, Mary's name is spun,
A kaleidoscope of verses under the radiant sun.
Her initials, like constellations in the night,
Guide the pen's journey with celestial light.
    Oh, Mary, the oracle of tales untold,
A narrative in every letter, a story to unfold.
Through the corridors of time, your echoes resound,
A symphony of syllables, profound.

In the garden of language, Mary's a bloom,
A fragrant stanza, dispelling gloom.
Her name, an incantation in the poet's quill,
A magical elixir, ever tranquil.

So here's to Mary, in the cathedral of words,
A melody that lingers, like songbirds.
Her name, a treasure trove in the poet's chest,
A timeless sonnet, eternally blessed.

NINETEEN

YOU STAND

Mary, a sonnet etched in the cosmic scroll,
A melody of letters, a lyrical stroll.
In the symphony of syllables, she pirouettes,
A linguistic ballet where euphony begets.

    In the labyrinth of language, her name weaves,
A tapestry of verses, where magic conceives.
Majestic Mary, in the lexicon's embrace,
A poetic comet, leaving trails of grace.

    Her consonants, celestial sentinels above,
Guardians of meaning, a testament to love.
Through epochs and echoes, Mary's tale unfurls,
A kaleidoscope of dreams in myriad swirls.

    Oh, Mary, the seraphic scribe of sound,
Your name, a treasure trove, profound.

A quill dipped in stardust, poetry in flight,
In the celestial manuscript, your name alight.
    In the ballad of existence, she takes the lead,
A dance of syllables, where stories breed.
Mary, the luminary in the poet's quest,
A timeless sonnet, forever at rest.
    As the ink of time weaves through the page,
Mary, the anthem, transcending age.
A poetic legacy in the universe's span,
In the constellation of names, you stand.

TWENTY

MARY'S LIGHT

In the lexicon's dance, Mary takes the floor,
A cascade of syllables, an eternal encore.
Her name, a quiver in the poet's bow,
A lyrical symphony in the moon's soft glow.
   Majestic Mary, in the tapestry of rhyme,
A harmonious echo throughout space and time.
Each letter, a painter's brush in the cosmic art,
A masterpiece of language, a work of heart.
   In the garden of verses, Mary's a bloom,
A fragrant sonnet, dispelling all gloom.
Her name, an oracle in the poet's trance,
A celestial dance in the linguistic expanse.
   Oh, Mary, the serenade of whispered dreams,
In the river of syllables, your name gleams.
A lighthouse of meaning in the poet's sea,
Guiding the verses to eternity.

Through the corridors of language, Mary strides,
A journey of letters where meaning abides.
Her name, a phoenix rising in the poet's ink,
A testament to beauty in every linguistic link.
In the cosmic sonnet, Mary's the refrain,
A poetic legacy, unbroken chain.
A constellation of verses, forever bright,
In the universe of words, Mary's light.

TWENTY-ONE

MARY'S MELODY RINGS

In the symphony of lexicons, Mary's melody rings,
A cascade of notes, where linguistic beauty springs.
Her name, a voyage through celestial spheres,
A poetic tapestry unfurling, allaying fears.

Majestic Mary, in the garden of prose,
A flourishing blossom where eloquence flows.
Each syllable, a brushstroke in language's art,
A masterpiece composed, a poetic heart.

In the labyrinth of sonnets, Mary takes the lead,
A dance of words where meanings intercede.
Her name, a compass guiding the poet's quill,
A celestial rhythm, ever echoing still.

Oh, Mary, the aurora in the poet's night,
A celestial canvas adorned with light.

A sonnet sung by zephyrs, whispered in the air,
In the celestial theater, a star so rare.
   Through the verses of time, Mary's tale unfolds,
A narrative in echoes, in whispers it molds.
Her name, an anthem in the poet's ode,
A timeless ballad on life's linguistic road.
   In the cosmic ballroom, Mary twirls,
A dance of letters, where imagination swirls.
Her name, a serenade in the poet's rhyme,
A poetic legacy, transcending space and time.

TWENTY-TWO

SOARING HIGH

In the lexicon's embrace, Mary's tale is spun,
A lyrical odyssey, where verses are begun.
Her name, a compass in the poet's hands,
Navigating through stanzas, like shifting sands.

Majestic Mary, in the symphony of sounds,
A melodious echo, where meaning abounds.
Each letter, a note in the cosmic score,
A lyrical dance, forever to explore.

In the garden of language, Mary blooms,
A kaleidoscope of syllables, dispelling glooms.
Her name, a sonnet in the poet's quill,
A tapestry of dreams, woven with skill.

Oh, Mary, the serenade in the poet's night,
A celestial beacon, a shimmering light.
In the ballad of words, your name's refrain,
A poetic legacy, an everlasting chain.

Through the corridors of time, Mary strides,
A dance of echoes where meaning resides.
Her name, an anthem in the poet's song,
A harmonious rhythm, where verses belong.

In the cosmic verses, Mary takes flight,
A celestial journey in the poet's sight.
Her name, a constellation in the linguistic sky,
A poetic masterpiece, soaring high.

TWENTY-THREE

SING OF MARY

In the realm of celestial grace,
Resides a name of timeless embrace,
Mary, the harbinger of light,
In her presence, all shadows take flight.
  Her name, a melody of serenity,
A symphony of divine eternity,
In each syllable, a whispered prayer,
A tapestry of love beyond compare.
  Majestic Mary, the moon's soft glow,
Guiding souls through the night's shadow,
Her name a beacon in the storm,
A refuge, a haven, tender and warm.
  In the garden of words, her name blooms,
A fragrant blossom, dispelling gloom,
Each letter a petal, delicate and pure,
A testament to love that will endure.

Mary, the keeper of ancient lore,
Her name a key to wisdom's door,
In her presence, hearts find solace,
As she weaves destinies with grace.

Oh, Mary, in your name we find,
Hope and solace for humankind,
In every prayer, every sacred chant,
Your name echoes, a holy enchant.

So let us raise our voices high,
And sing of Mary, in the sky,
For in her name, we find our way,
Guided by her light, come what may.

TWENTY-FOUR

AGELESS YOUTH

Amidst the emerald meadows, Mary dances free,
Her name a whispered hymn, a melody of glee.
In every petal's bloom, in every rustling tree,
Her essence lingers, timeless, wild, and carefree.

In the depths of starlit oceans, Mary's name resounds,
A symphony of secrets, in the depths, she is found.
Each ripple, a verse, each wave, a sacred vow,
Her name a lullaby, to calm the tempest's growl.

Marvelous Mary, in twilight's silken embrace,
Her name ignites the heavens, a celestial grace.
In every flickering candle, in every twilight spark,
Her name kindles hope, in the abyss, so dark.

Oh, Mary, in your name, a universe unfurls,
A tapestry of wonders, a constellation of pearls.

In every whispered prayer, in every tender plea,
Your name holds the key to a world yet to be.

In the cathedral of dreams, Mary's name ascends,
A celestial dance, where eternity transcends.
Each echo, a promise, each whisper, a sacred art,
Her name a beacon of love, in every beating heart.

So let us raise our voices, and sing of Mary's name,
A symphony of grace, a wildfire, untamed.
For in her name, we find solace, in her name, we find our truth,
Guided by her light, through the endless, ageless youth.

TWENTY-FIVE

CELEBRATED, ADORED, AND ADORED

Mary, maiden of the morning mist,
Majestic in her grace, a marvel to behold,
Mirthful melodies dance upon her lips,
Mystic aura surrounds her, a tale untold.

Majestic Mary, mistress of the moonlit sky,
Mystifying in her ways, a mosaic of light,
Mirthful laughter fills the air, a melody so high,
Mesmerizing all who behold her, a wondrous sight.

Majestic Mary, muse of the mountain peaks,
Mystical in her movements, a mesmerizing dance,
Mirthful whispers in the wind, a melody that speaks,
Mesmerizing all who witness, a timeless romance.

Majestic Mary, monarch of the meadows fair,

Mystical in her presence, a miracle to see,
Mirthful joy in her heart, a melody rare,
Mesmerizing all who know her, a symphony so free.

Majestic Mary, maiden of magnificence,
Mystical in her essence, a masterpiece divine,
Mirthful spirit that shines, a melody of transcendence,
Mesmerizing all who love her, a treasure to enshrine.

Mary, a name that echoes through the ages,
Majestic, mystical, mirthful, and more,
A beacon of light in history's pages,
Forever celebrated, adored, and adored.

TWENTY-SIX

MAGNIFICENT AND MAJESTIC

Majestic Mary, maiden of grace,
Mirthful and merry, with a radiant face.
Mystical and magical, her name doth ring,
Mellifluous melodies, as the angels sing.

Marvelous Mary, in the moonlit night,
Moonbeams shimmer, casting a gentle light,
Magnificent and majestic, her spirit soars,
Majestic mountains, and distant shores.

Majestic Mary, a muse of the mind,
Mystical musings, that are one of a kind,
Mirthful and merry, like a babbling brook,
Magnetic and mesmerizing, with every look.

Majestic Mary, with a heart of gold,
Mirthful laughter, that never grows old,

Mellifluous voice, that soothes the soul,
Magical moments, that make us whole.

Majestic Mary, in the meadow green,
Mirthful and merry, a sight to be seen,
Mystical and mysterious, like a hidden gem,
Majestic and marvelous, a rare diadem.

Majestic Mary, under the morning sky,
Mirthful and merry, as the birds fly high,
Magnificent and majestic, in every way,
Majestic Mary, forever and a day.

Majestic Mary, with a spirit so free,
Mirthful and merry, like the dancing sea,
Majestic and magical, in every way,
Majestic Mary, forever and a day.

TWENTY-SEVEN

PRECIOUS PEARL

Mary, oh radiant star of the night,
In your name, there's a shimmering light,
A melody of grace and beauty combined,
A symphony of elegance, one of a kind.

Majestic Mary, queen of the skies,
With your name, the heavens arise,
A constellation of love and kindness,
A tapestry of hope and forgiveness.

Marvellous Mary, with a heart so pure,
Your name echoes like a celestial lure,
A sanctuary of peace and tranquility,
A haven of serenity and humility.

Mirthful Mary, with laughter so sweet,
In your name, joy and happiness meet,
A carnival of laughter and delight,
A jubilee of merriment, shining bright.

Magnificent Mary, in your name we find,
A treasure trove of virtues intertwined,
A kaleidoscope of virtues and grace,
A mosaic of love that time can't erase.

Oh Mary, your name is a divine art,
A masterpiece that captures every heart,
In your name, a universe of wonders unfurl,
A masterpiece, the epitome of a precious pearl.

TWENTY-EIGHT

PURE AND RARE

Majestic Mary, in your name, a symphony of stars,
A tapestry of dreams, weaving through the night,
A radiant beacon, guiding souls from afar,
A celestial dance, shimmering with pure delight.
Mystical Mary, with a spirit wild and free,
In your name, there's a melody that never fades,
A dance of moonbeams, across the endless sea,
A serenade of whispers, in enchanted glades.
Marvelous Mary, with a heart so full of light,
In your name, there's a sanctuary of solace,
A haven of hope, burning through the darkest night,
A garden of grace, where weary souls find solace.
Melodic Mary, with laughter like a summer breeze,
In your name, there's a carnival of joyous sound,
A symposium of mirth, beneath the swaying trees,
A jubilant chorus, where happiness abounds.

Oh Mary, your name is a treasure, pure and rare,
A masterpiece of love that time can never mar,
In your name, a universe of wonders to declare,
A radiant beacon, guiding us to where you are.

TWENTY-NINE

HAIL TO THEE

Hail to thee, fair Mary, with grace so divine,
In a world of chaos, your name doth shine.
Majestic and serene, like a gentle breeze,
In your presence, the soul finds peace.
Your name, a symphony of elegance and charm,
A melody that soothes, a balm for the harm.
In the tapestry of life, you're a radiant thread,
A beacon of hope, where darkness has fled.
Mary, the muse of poets and artists alike,
Your name evokes beauty, a celestial spike.
In the garden of words, you bloom like a rose,
A fragrance that lingers, wherever it goes.
Oh, Mary, a name that echoes through time,
A legacy of love, a rhythm and rhyme.
In the corridors of history, your name stands tall,
A testament to grace, for one and all.

So here's to you, Mary, a name so sublime,
In the lexicon of life, a jewel that's prime.
May your name be cherished, forevermore,
A treasure to behold, a name to adore.

THIRTY

MILLION STARS

Majestic Mary, muse of the morn,
In your name, a melody is born.
Mystical and mesmerizing, like the moon's glow,
Your essence weaves through time, a timeless flow.
Mirthful Mary, maiden of the meadow,
In your name, nature's beauty is bestowed.
Mystifying and magical, like a murmuring stream,
Your presence dances through dreams, a radiant beam.
Magnificent Mary, monarch of the mountains,
In your name, a symphony of serenity encounters.
Mystique and meaningful, like a murmuring breeze,
Your spirit whispers through the world, a tranquil tease.
Mindful Mary, mentor of the moonbeams,
In your name, a masterpiece of meaning gleams.

Mystical and melodious, like a midnight choir,
Your wisdom resonates through hearts, a celestial fire.
    Majestic Mary, your name a marvel of marvels,
In your honor, our voices rise and marvel.
Mystical and majestic, like a million stars,
Your legacy shines through eternity, a celestial memoir.

THIRTY-ONE

REGAL BEAUTY

Of regal beauty, she stands, Mary,
A name as timeless as the stars,
In her gaze, the cosmos unwinds,
A symphony of grace and light.

Mary, the harbinger of hope,
Her name a melody in the wind,
Whispered by the ancients,
Carried on the wings of time.

In her name, a garden blooms,
Petals unfurling in reverence,
Each one a verse of love,
Penned by the hand of eternity.

Mary, the empress of dreams,
Her name a tapestry of wonder,
Woven with threads of destiny,
An ode to the divine feminine.

In her name, the oceans dance,
Their waves a chorus of adoration,
Sung to the rhythm of her heartbeat,
A serenade to the soul of the world.

Mary, the guardian of secrets,
Her name a sanctuary of whispers,
Where echoes of ancient wisdom reside,
A sanctuary for the seekers of truth.

In her name, the stars align,
Their constellations a tribute,
To the enigma of her essence,
A celestial ode to her boundless spirit.

Mary, the muse of poets,
Her name a sonnet of enchantment,
A verse that transcends time,
A lyrical homage to her infinite majesty.

THIRTY-TWO

LOVE AND PEACE

Of all the names that grace the earth,
Mary, you boast a regal worth.
A moniker so sweet and fine,
With echoes of a grand design.

In gardens fair and fields of green,
Your name is heard, a gentle sheen.
It dances on the lips with grace,
A melody in time and space.

Majestic Mary, noble and true,
Your name brings visions, old and new.
A symphony of syllables,
A tapestry of miracles.

In whispered prayers and solemn hymns,
Your name ascends on seraphim's wings.
It weaves a spell of peace and light,
A beacon in the darkest night.

From ancient lands to modern days,
Your name endures in countless ways.
A cornerstone of history's tale,
A lighthouse in a stormy gale.
   Oh Mary, name of timeless fame,
In every heart, you leave your claim.
A melody that will not cease,
A legacy of love and peace.

THIRTY-THREE

BOUNDARIES OF TIME

In the symphony of night, where shadows weave,
Mary, a name, a celestial reprieve.
Her essence, a sonnet in twilight's embrace,
A dance of stardust, a cosmic grace.
Beneath the moon's silvery cascade,
Mary, a melody in the celestial parade.
A serenade sung by zephyrs at play,
Her name, a comet's journey in the astral ballet.
Gardens of dreams where Mary strolls,
In the cosmic ballad, her spirit controls.
A tapestry woven with threads of starlight,
Her name, a radiant beacon in the cosmic night.
Moonlit verses etched on the celestial scroll,
Mary, a lyric, a seraphic soul.

Through galaxies, her name takes flight,
In the cosmic tapestry, a radiant light.
    Oh, Mary, in the celestial verse,
A name that the universe warmly rehearse.
Her name, a lullaby in the stellar breeze,
A symphony of stars, a celestial tease.
    Her presence, a constellation in the cosmic dome,
A luminous lyric, forever to roam.
Majestic Mary, in the cosmic rhyme,
A name that transcends the boundaries of time.

THIRTY-FOUR

DAY AND NIGHT

Hail, Mary, in your splendor bright,
A name that shines with pure delight.
In whispers soft and anthems bold,
Your essence weaves a tale untold.

Majestic Mary, in the morning dew,
Your name sparkles with a golden hue.
It echoes through the emerald glades,
And dances in the secret shades.

In ancient tomes and modern lore,
Your name resounds forevermore.
A symphony of timeless grace,
A treasure in the human race.

In sacred chants and solemn vows,
Your name ascends on sacred boughs.
It paints a picture, vivid and clear,
A solace for the weary ear.

  Oh Mary, name of ancient lore,
Your beauty opens every door.
A melody that cannot fade,
A tribute to the serenade.
  In every heart, your name abides,
A beacon in the ebbing tides.
A legacy of love and light,
A symphony of day and night.

THIRTY-FIVE

HAVEN OF HOPE

Mary, the maiden of grace and light,
Her name a melody, a symphony of delight.
In realms of reverie, her spirit soars,
A seraphic being, with wisdom that adores.
Majestic Mary, with eyes like sapphire seas,
Her presence a balm, a celestial ease.
Mirthful and merry, her laughter cascades,
A jubilant echo in verdant glades.
Mystical Mary, with a heart aglow,
In her embrace, all troubles ebb and flow.
Her words, like honey, sweeten the air,
A benediction, a solace rare.
Mellifluous Mary, her voice a lullaby,
Whispering secrets, neath the cerulean sky.
In her name, a sanctuary is found,
A haven of hope, where joy knows no bound.

Magnificent Mary, in every petal's bloom,
Her essence pervades, dispelling all gloom.
In her name, a symphony of stars align,
A celestial dance, where dreams intertwine.

Marvelous Mary, in her name we find,
A tapestry of grace, ever intertwined.
In every syllable, a universe unfurls,
A hymn of love, where eternity twirls.

Majestic, mystical, mellifluous Mary,
In her name, a timeless sanctuary,
A beacon of light, in the darkest night,
A sublime testament, to love's resplendent might.

ABOUT THE AUTHOR

Walter the Educator is one of the pseudonyms for Walter Anderson. Formally educated in Chemistry, Business, and Education, he is an educator, an author, a diverse entrepreneur, and he is the son of a disabled war veteran. "Walter the Educator" shares his time between educating and creating. He holds interests and owns several creative projects that entertain, enlighten, enhance, and educate, hoping to inspire and motivate you.

Follow, find new works, and stay up to date
with Walter the Educator™
at WaltertheEducator.com

www.ingramcontent.com/pod-product-compliance
Lightning Source LLC
LaVergne TN
LVHW010603070526
838199LV00063BA/5058